LITTLE ELEPHANT

© 2022 Quarto Publishing Group USA Inc.
Text © 2022 Anna Brett
Illustrations © 2022 Carmen Saldaña

First published in 2022 by QEB Publishing,
an imprint of The Quarto Group.
100 Cummings Center,
Suite 265D Beverly, MA 01915, USA.
T (978) 282-9590 F (978) 283-2742
www.quarto.com

Editorial Assistant: Alice Hobbs
Art Director: Susi Martin
Publisher: Holly Willsher

A CIP record for this book is available from the Library of Congress.

ISBN: 978-0-7112-7412-9

9 8 7 6 5 4 3 2

Manufactured in Guangdong, China TT052023

MIX
Paper | Supporting
responsible forestry
FSC
www.fsc.org
FSC® C016973

LITTLE ELEPHANT

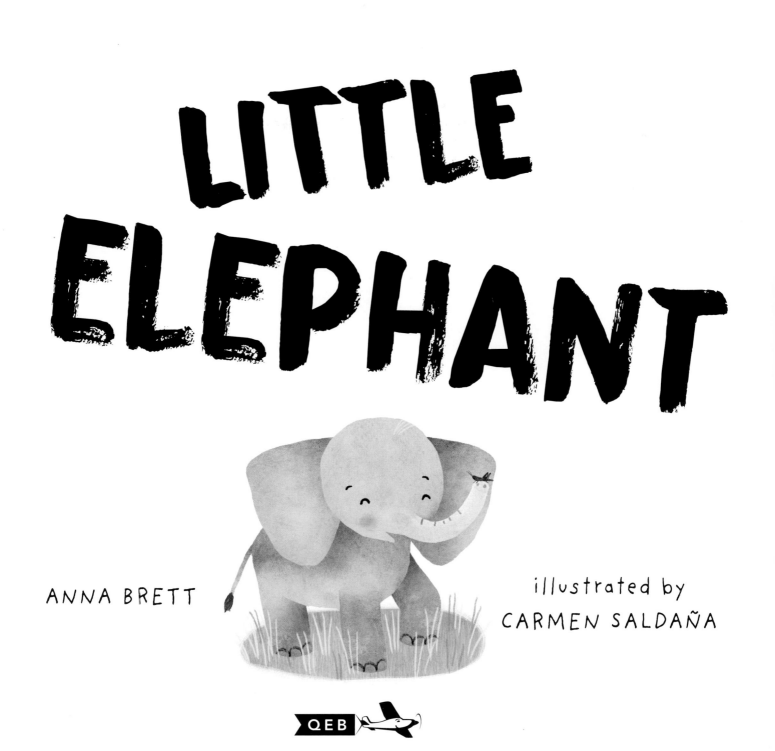

ANNA BRETT

illustrated by
CARMEN SALDAÑA

QEB

Hello, I'm Little Elephant and this is my mommy and grandma. I'm proud to say we're the world's largest land mammals—although I've still got a bit more growing to do!

Our family group is called a herd.
Come and spend the day with us.

We live on the African savanna.

There are fifteen of us in our family herd. We're all female apart from my two young male cousins. Our beloved grandma is over 60 years old and she is head of the herd. She is very wise and loves telling us about all the wonderful things she's experienced in life.

Grandma has such long tusks!
They have been growing a long time.

I'm always hungry!
Our stomachs are huge so we
need to eat lots and lots to fill
them. We gobble the leaves
and branches off bushes and
trees, but my favorite foods
are fruit and fresh grass.

It's dawn at the moment, so the cooler temperatures mean we can head off for a nice walk in search of breakfast.

Our home is on the grasslands of the African savanna. My family roams over hundreds of miles looking for food and water. Grandma shows us the way, since she has walked across most of it over her lifetime!

We share our habitat with many other animals, including these playful oxpecker birds.

When we set off for a long walk, we all march in single file. I need to hold on to Mommy's tail to help me keep up!

Grandma leads the way, and she can figure out what's happening nearby by feeling the vibrations in the ground through her feet.

Our walk has brought us to the watering hole. I love it here. There's always time for fun as well as a drink. We use our trunks to suck up water...and to spray it!

Trunks are an extension of our nose and top lip.

Mommy is also using her trunk like a snorkel so she can enjoy a swim.

Yippee, it's bath time—but our baths
involve mud instead of water!

We love to splash cool mud and scratchy sand over our skin. It protects us from sunburn and insect bites.

Time for some roly-poly fun with my cousins while Grandma keeps watch.

As we turn to leave the watering hole, Mommy stops to tell us about a male we can see. He, like all male elephants, left the female herd when he became a teenager so he could become more independent.

Some elephants have learned to stand on their back legs to reach the very highest leaves.

Come and meet my baby cousin.
She was born just two days ago.
She's very cute...and clever.

Mommy elephants are pregnant for
a long time—22 months in total.

She could stand up within 20 minutes of being born, and started walking after an hour.

Now she can even keep up with the herd so we can continue moving across the savanna.

21

Uh-oh, Grandma has sounded
the alarm with a loud trumpet call.
There's a lion nearby.

Lions can run much faster than us, so our best form of defense is to huddle together. The adults form a circle around us calves to keep us safe and close.

The danger has passed and the lion has gone. We elephants are peaceful animals, but if we do need to defend ourselves our tusks come in handy.

Tusks are huge teeth
that start growing out
from our upper jaw after
the age of two.

They are useful for
digging, lifting, and
gathering food as well.

We love to chat, and have many ways of doing this.
Trumpeting through our trunk is fun, but deep
growls and rumbles are our common chatter.
We also flap our ears and stamp our feet
to let our family know what's happening.

Our powerful low rumbles
can be heard far away, so
this helps us locate anyone
missing from the herd.

27

Phew, it's getting hot! Luckily our huge floppy ears help us stay cool.

Their size helps heat escape from our bodies, and flapping them works like a fan. We are African elephants and our ears are shaped like the continent on which we live!

29

My mommy is so caring. She takes care of me
and everyone in the herd.

When my aunt hurt her leg, she nursed
her back to full strength and we all walked
slower so she could keep up.

I learn so much from her
every day and we love to
hug each other by wrapping
our trunks together.

It's been a busy day and we all need to rest for a few hours now. Mommy stays standing up for her nap, but I prefer to lie down.

Sometimes Grandma will stay
awake all night to keep watch
over us so we can sleep soundly.

Goodnight, everyone!

FUN FACTS

I hope you enjoyed being a member of our herd for the day!

African savanna elephant.

Stay with us for a little longer and I'll tell you even more about elephants.

- There are three different species of elephant: the African savanna elephant, the African forest elephant, and the Asian elephant.

- African elephants have two "fingers" at the end of their trunk, Asian elephants have one.

- Baby elephants are called calves, females are called cows and males are called bulls.

- Elephants need to eat up to 330 lbs of food a day.

- They need to drink 30-60 gallons of water a day.

- Elephants have very good memories.

- Elephants are afraid of bees!

Babies are born without tusks.

Elephants are herbivores.

FACT FILE

Height: Up to 10 feet

Weight: Up to 6.6 tons (babies are born weighing a huge 265 lbs!)

Speed: Top speed – 19 mph, walking speed – 4 mph

Lifespan: Up to 70 years

FOLLOW THE FOOTPRINTS

This family is setting off for a walk across the savanna.
Can you spot which of them is the odd one out in the herd?

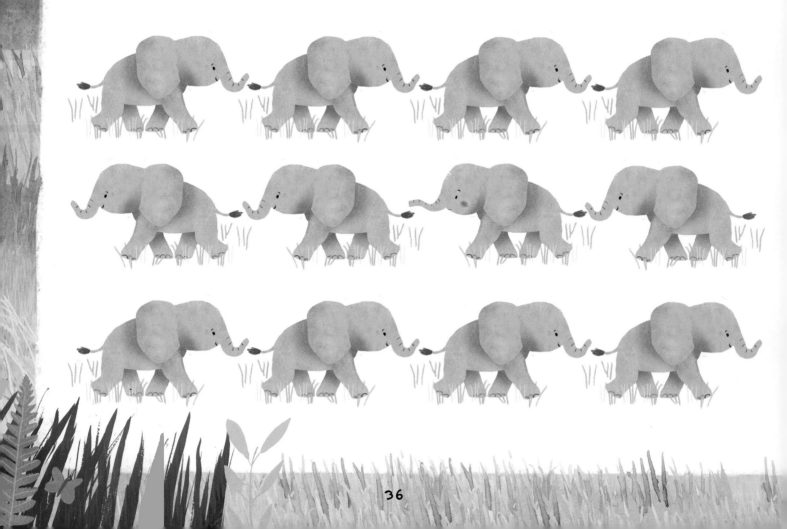

The elephants have arrived at the waterhole and are enjoying splashing in the muddy puddles! Can you tell which trail each elephant took to reach the mud?

CONSERVATION

Sadly, numbers of elephants in the wild are in decline. They are listed as an endangered species. In particular the number of African forest elephants has dropped by over 80% in 30 years.

A small herd of elephants safely walking in the Tsavo National Park, Kenya.

The elephant population is threatened by hunting and habitat loss. But conservation is the way humans can help protect the world's largest land animals. Banning the hunting of elephants and educating people on how to protect the habitat and live alongside these magnificent mammals will hopefully mean numbers can grow again in the future.

A great example of conservation is the way that people are coming up with new, safe ways to reduce the conflict between elephants and farmers. Elephants may wander onto farmland in search of food, but this upsets the farmers who don't want to lose their crops. So conservationists have discovered that, since elephants don't like bees, setting up a fence of beehives around crops works as a natural deterrent! This has worked with real success in Sagalla, next to the Tsavo East National Park in Kenya.

A farmer inspects his beehive fence in Sagalla, Kenya.

Although a bee sting can't get through the thick skin of an elephant, it can really hurt their eyes, trunk, and mouth. And African bees are known to be aggressive when they swarm. So despite their size difference, it's easy to understand why elephants dislike them!

FOOD AND FAMILY

It's lunchtime for these elephants. Their long trunks allow them to reach up to get the highest leaves! Which jigsaw piece completes the picture?

a

b

c

Elephant calves stay close to their mommies whilst they are young. But this group has become a bit muddled. Can you help each baby find its mommy by matching them up?

a

b

c

d

1

2

3

4

CRAFT ACTIVITY

Follow these steps to make an elephant with a tremendous moving trunk!

- A square piece of gray paper (or any other color you'd like your elephant to be!)
- Glue
- A paper straw
- A long rectangular piece of gray paper (or any other color you'd like your trunk to be!)
- A black pen
- A piece of white paper
- Scissors

1 Fold your square piece of paper in half diagonally and then cut along the fold to create two triangles.

2 Fold down the top tip of both triangles a few centimetres. Take one triangle and add glue down the center so you can stick the straw in position as shown.

3 Add glue to the paper on both sides of the straw and then stick one end of your rectangular piece of paper over the straw. This will be the elephant's trunk.

4 Glue all over the rest of this first triangle and then carefully position the second triangle over the top and press down.

5 Take your pen and roll the bottom of the trunk around it. You need to place the pen and roll the side of the paper that has the straw stuck to it!

6 Next, fold down the outer corners of the triangle to create the ears.

7 Cut out two long triangle shapes from the white piece of paper to create the tusks, then glue into position. Remember, the older the elephant, the longer the tusks!

8 Finally, use the black pen to draw the eyes and add some wrinkle lines to the trunk. Now blow down the straw to see your paper elephant's mighty trunk move!

CASE STUDY

The Reteti Elephant Sanctuary in Northern Kenya is the first community owned elephant sanctuary in Africa. Opened in 2016, it rescues, rehabilitates, and then releases orphaned or abandoned elephant calves back to their family herds in the wild.

A herd of rescued young elephants at the Reteti Elephant Sanctuary.

It is run by the local Samburu community, which means jobs are created for locals. This is a great step for conservation, since it teaches the locals about these magnificent creatures, creates a stable income for them, and protects the natural habitat from development.

Young calves may be orphaned due to drought, getting stuck in man-made water wells, human-wildlife conflict, or just natural occurrences. The sanctuary has a mobile rescue team that can travel where needed to help rescue them.

The keepers and young elephants often form a strong bond.

A keeper feeds an orphaned elephant with a bottle of milk.

Once a calf has been rescued, the keepers at the sanctuary feed it milk until it is old enough for solid food. When the calf is at full strength, it is moved to the Sera Wildlife Conservancy habitat where it can interact with wild elephants once again. After that they may then leave the Sera area altogether to become truly wild.

QUIZ

See how much you've learned about elephants by testing your knowledge with these fun questions.

1. What is a group of elephants called?

2. True or false: elephants are born with tusks.

3. Which insect do elephants not like?

4. Do elephants use one, two, or all of these as a form of communication? Trumpet call, flapping ears, foot stamping.

5. True or false: a female elephant is called a bull.

6. Do elephants flap their tails or their ears to cool themselves down?

7. True or false: elephants eat meat.

8. Elephants can be found in the wild on which two continents?

9. Elephants like to wash themselves in water and what else?

10. Does the oldest female or the oldest male elephant lead the group?

The answers are on the next page.

ANSWERS

P36-37

a=2 b=3 c=1

P40-41

a=3, b=2, c=4, d=1

Quiz Answers

1. A herd
2. False
3. Bees
4. All three of these are used as ways to communicate!
5. False—a female is called a cow
6. Ears
7. False—they only eat plants
8. Africa and Asia
9. Mud
10. The oldest female. She's called the matriarch of the family